MILESTONES
IN MODERN SCIENCE

THE FIRST
POLIO VACCINE

Guy de la Bédoyère

Evans

Published by Evans Brothers Limited
2A Portman Mansions
Chiltern Street
London W1U 6NR

© Evans Brothers Limited 2005

First published 2005

British Library Cataloguing in Publication Data

De la Bedoyere, Guy
The first polio vaccine. - (Milestones in modern science)
    1. Poliomyelitis vaccine – History – Juvenile literature
    2. Poliomyelitis – Vaccination – History – Juvenile literature
    3. Discoveries in science – Juvenile literature
    I. Title
615. 5'49

ISBN 0237527383

Consultant: Dr Anne Whitehead
Editor: Sonya Newland
Designer: D.R. Ink, info@d-r-ink.com
Picture researcher: Julia Bird

Acknowledgements

Cover National Library of Medicine/Science Photo Library; Science Museum/Science & Society Picture Library; James King-Holmes/Science Photo Library **3** Bettmann/Corbis **4(t)** TopFoto.co.uk **4(b)** National Museum of Photography, Film & Television/Daily Herald Archive/Science & Society Picture Library **5** Science Museum/Science & Society Picture Library **6** Jean-Loup Charmet/Science Photo Library **7** Science Photo Library **8(t)** Science Photo Library **8(b)** Stanley B. Burns, MD & the Burns Archive N.Y./Science Photo Library **9(t)** St Bartholomew's Hospital/Science Photo Library **9(b)** Science Photo Library **10** Jean-Loup Charmet/Science Photo Library **11** National Library of Medicine/Science Photo Library **12(t)** Science Museum/Science & Society Picture Library **12(b)** Jean-Loup Charmet/Science Photo Library **13(t)** Science Museum/Science & Society Picture Library **13(b)** Sheila Terry/Science Photo Library **14** Biophoto Associates/Science Photo Library **17** Science Museum/Science & Society Picture Library **18** Stanley B. Burns, MD & the Burns Archive N.Y./Science Photo Library **19(t)** Science Photo Library **19(b)** Stanley B. Burns, MD & the Burns Archive N.Y./Science Photo Library **20** © Bettmann/Corbis **21** James King-Holmes/Science Photo Library **22** TopFoto.co.uk **23(t)** © Bettmann/Corbis **23(b)** TopFoto.co.uk **24(t)** National Library of Medicine/Science Photo Library **25(t)** Custom Medical Stock Photo/Science Photo Library **25(b)** CDC/Science Photo Library **26** National Library of Medicine/Science Photo Library **27** TopFoto.co.uk **28** Stanley B. Burns, MD & the Burns Archive N.Y./Science Photo Library **29(t)** National Library of Medicine/Science Photo Library **29(b)** © Bettmann/Corbis **30** © Bettmann/Corbis **31** © Bettmann/Corbis **32** © Bettmann/Corbis **33** © Bettmann/Corbis **34** © Bettmann/Corbis **35(t)** National Library of Medicine/Science Photo Library **36 (background)** CDC/Science Photo Library **36 (inset)** © Bettmann/Corbis **37** Saturn Stills/Science Photo Library **38(t)** © Rafiqur Rahman/Reuters/Corbis **38(b)** Science Museum/Science & Society Picture Library **40** S. Nagendra/Science Photo Library **41(l)** © Steve Raymer/Corbis **41(r)** Russell Kightley/Science Photo Library **42** Lowell Georgia/Science Photo Library **43(l)** Chris Priest & Mark Clarke/Science Photo Library **43(r)** Health Education Authority/Science & Society Picture Library **44** TopFoto.co.uk

CONTENTS

◆ INTRODUCTION...4

◆ CHAPTER ONE
**Early Experiments
with Vaccines** 6

◆ CHAPTER TWO
The Polio Virus 14

◆ CHAPTER THREE
Salk's Investigations 24

◆ CHAPTER FOUR
**The Vaccine Works!
Field Tests and Mass Trials**......30

◆ CHAPTER FIVE
New Vaccines 34

◆ CHAPTER SIX
Polio Today 38

◆ TIMELINE 44

◆ GLOSSARY 45

◆ FURTHER INFORMATION 47

◆ INDEX 48

ENTRANCE

for polio shots

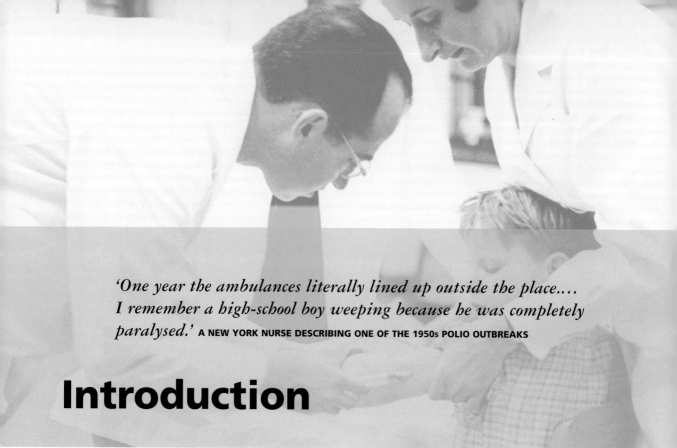

'One year the ambulances literally lined up outside the place.... I remember a high-school boy weeping because he was completely paralysed.' **A NEW YORK NURSE DESCRIBING ONE OF THE 1950s POLIO OUTBREAKS**

Introduction

ABOVE: *In this photo, taken in 1957, a young boy winces as Jonas Salk injects him with a dose of the vaccine he developed.*

BELOW: *Polio can cause paralysis of the muscles in the chest. In 1938, when this picture was taken, the only way to treat this was to use an 'iron lung', a machine that helped polio sufferers breathe.*

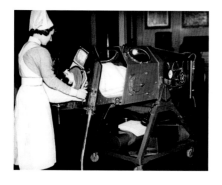

Polio is a terrible disease that can paralyse limbs, cause brain damage and, in extreme cases, result in death. In the early to mid twentieth century, epidemics of the disease ravaged countries like the United States, causing widespread panic and striking fear into the heart of the population. Nobody knew what caused it or how it spread. There were no effective treatments for people who caught polio and there was certainly no cure. Although many people recovered from the disease, they could be paralysed or blinded, and would have to live the rest of their lives with the effects of polio. Doctors and scientists had to find some way of preventing the disease.

Edward Jenner had created a smallpox vaccine in the late eighteenth century, and since this time, doctors and scientists had known that in some cases, exposing people to very small doses of a virus could result in immunity from the disease it caused. The doses were not enough to create a full-blown case of the disease; they were just enough for the body to create antibodies that would fight back should the virus attack properly. These scientists wondered if polio could be prevented using a similar method.

The situation reached crisis point in the late 1930s, and the US president, Franklin D. Roosevelt, established the National Foundation for Infantile Paralysis in 1938 to raise funds to start research into a polio vaccine. So great was people's terror of the illness and so dire was the need to find a way of preventing it that donations came flooding in. Now all they needed was someone to lead the research. The man they turned to was Jonas Salk.

The problem with polio, as Salk soon discovered, was that it came in several different forms, each caused by a different type of virus. To make an effective vaccine, Salk's team would have to find something that could fight all three types. It was a daunting task and public pressure to find a vaccine was high. Despite the difficulties, they created a vaccine with remarkable speed, and Salk was hailed as a hero as the country celebrated. This was not the end of the story, though. There were more hurdles to overcome, and other scientists who were working on better, more effective vaccines against polio. These included Albert Sabin, who had a low opinion of Salk's methods and the vaccine he produced.

Even today, people disagree about whether Sabin's vaccine is better than Salk's – and each have had times of being the favoured method of inoculation against the disease. Although Salk is remembered as the man who brought polio under control, the contribution of other scientists, especially Sabin, should not be underestimated. Thanks to the dedication and perseverance of these people, we are now in a situation that would have seemed like an impossibility 50 years ago – we are standing on the brink of a polio-free world.

ABOVE: *Using kits like this, health organisations are working on vaccination programmes worldwide in an effort to eliminate polio altogether in the next few years.*

CHAPTER ONE

'I hope that one day the practice of producing cowpox in human beings will spread over the world – when that day comes, there will be no more smallpox.' EDWARD JENNER, c. 1798

Early Experiments with Vaccines

ABOVE: *In the seventeenth century, plague was the most feared disease across Europe. Victims experienced high fevers and aches, accompanied by large painful boils. We now know that the organism that caused the plague was carried by fleas that lived on rats, and it was passed to humans through flea bites. The disease spread like wildfire and thousands of people died. This picture shows plague victims being collected for burial.*

FOR THOUSANDS OF YEARS HUMANS HAVE tried to combat disease and infection. Unfortunately, without understanding the cause, treatment was largely guesswork and often ineffective. More importantly, preventing disease was almost impossible. This began to change in the seventeenth century, when severe outbreaks of diseases like plague, cholera and smallpox forced doctors and scientists to work hard to find new methods of preventing these deadly infections.

TRADITIONAL MEDICINE

For many centuries, treatments for disease were usually based on observation and folklore, but this was not as primitive as it sounds. There were doctors in ancient Egypt and during the time of the Roman Empire, and surgery for wounds received in battle, chariot races and gladiatorial fights was highly developed. It was infections that perplexed physicians. They did not understand why diseases such as cholera and plague

Key People

Paracelsus (c. 1493–1541) was a Swiss physician who pioneered alchemy in medicine. Alchemy was the search for hidden powers in substances that would bring health and prosperity, and it was based on the idea that materials with similar properties or similar effects had a powerful, almost magical, relationship. Although some of his ideas seem strange to us now, Paracelsus's theories were advanced for their time. He challenged the belief that Greek and Roman medical writings were always correct. He suggested the use of specific remedies for specific diseases; for example he used mercury to treat syphilis and he also used opium as a medicine because it relieved pain.

occurred and spread so rapidly. The ancient Roman scholar Marcus Terrentius Varro (116–27 BC) speculated that malaria was caused by minute animals in water, but there was no proof for this theory.

The mystery remained for centuries, and even in the 1600s, little was understood about what caused infectious diseases like plague and smallpox. These were two of the deadliest diseases at this time. Outbreaks of plague occurred across Europe and there was no treatment. In London in 1665, 100,000 people – about 25 per cent of the population – died in the last major outbreak of plague. Smallpox was also common, affecting rich and poor, and no one had any idea that it was caused by a virus, or how to prevent it. Queen Mary II, joint ruler of Britain with her husband William III, died of the disease when she was only 32 years old.

NEW SCIENCE

By this time, however, scientific thought was changing. The microscope had been invented in 1609 and this opened up a whole new world of discovery, as people were able to see things that had not previously been visible to the naked eye. Scientists exchanged new ideas instead of relying on Greek and Roman books.

Fact

SMALLPOX
After an incubation period of 12 days, victims of smallpox got headaches, high temperatures and pains in their back and limbs. Three days later spots would break out. Many victims survived with bad scars, but some were blinded – many died. Today the disease has disappeared; the last cases were seen in the late 1970s and in 1980 the World Health Organization announced that smallpox had been completely eradicated from our world.

Key People

Samuel Hahnemann (1755–1843) was a German doctor greatly influenced by the works of Paracelsus (see p. 7). He was frustrated by the medical practices of his age, and started to investigate different diseases and possible treatments. He found that the drug quinine seemed to cure malaria, an illness that caused a high fever, shaking and headaches. However, he also spotted that the drug itself actually caused symptoms very similar to those of disease. Hahnemann called this his 'Law of Similars', a principle that had its origins in alchemy. Quinine was the first successful use of a chemical compound against infectious disease.

BELOW: A vaccination experiment on a cow in the nineteenth century. Cowpox was similar to smallpox, and Edward Jenner showed that by infecting humans with cowpox, which was only a mild disease, they gained an immunity to the more dangerous smallpox.

Investigating the causes of disease became the driving force behind the new science of microscopic study.

In the early 1700s travellers from Turkey brought stories to Britain and America about the use of fluid from smallpox pustules to protect against the disease. This practice was called variolation, meaning 'to infect with

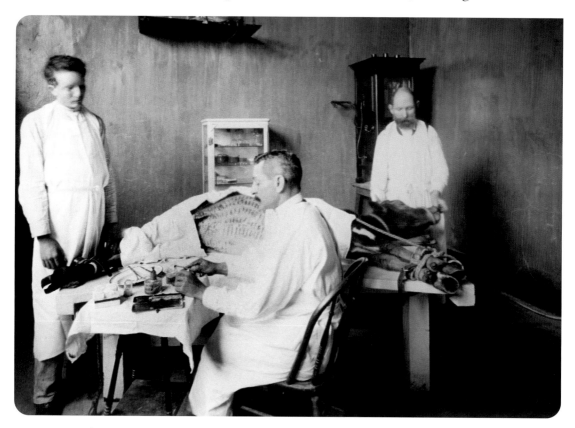

AN

INQUIRY

INTO

THE CAUSES AND EFFECTS

OF

THE VARIOLÆ VACCINÆ,

A DISEASE

DISCOVERED IN SOME OF THE WESTERN COUNTIES OF ENGLAND,

PARTICULARLY

GLOUCESTERSHIRE,

AND KNOWN BY THE NAME OF

THE COW POX.

BY EDWARD JENNER, M.D. F.R.S. &c.

——— QUID NOBIS CERTIUS IPSIS

SENSIBUS ESSE POTEST, QUO VERA AC FALSA NOTEMUS.

LUCRETIUS.

London:

PRINTED, FOR THE AUTHOR,

BY SAMPSON LOW, Nº. 7, BERWICK STREET, SOHO:

AND SOLD BY LAW, AVE-MARIA LANE; AND MURRAY AND HIGHLEY, FLEET STREET.

LEFT: *Jenner published the results of his findings about cowpox in 1798, but in the course of his experiments some people still became infected with smallpox. This was enough for scientists to scorn Jenner's beliefs about vaccination.*

BELOW: *Lady Mary Wortley Montagu had lived in Turkey, where they used a method of inoculation called variolation. People were injected with a dose of smallpox and in many instances it prevented the full-blown disease taking hold. Lady Mary introduced the practice to England on her return, and it had a measure of success, although it was still risky.*

smallpox'. In 1718 Lady Mary Wortley Montagu (1689–1762), the wife of the British ambassador in Constantinople, Turkey, returned to England and introduced the practice of variolation. Of course, to begin with, people were wary of trying out this new method, so prisoners were experimented on to see if it worked. The trials were successful and the practice became common in high society; even members of the British royal family were inoculated. Variolation was not an ideal solution, however, because there was always a chance that the patient could catch full-blown smallpox.

THE GREAT COWPOX DISCOVERY

Edward Jenner was very interested in the practice of variolation and had read about Hahnemann's studies and the 'Law of Similars', whereby the application of certain substances caused similar symptoms to the disease it prevented, although they were

Key People

Edward Jenner (1749–1823) had worked as an army doctor and then became a country doctor in Gloucestershire, England. In May 1796 a milkmaid called Sarah Nelmes came to see him. Sarah had a cowpox rash on her hand. Jenner saw his chance to prove that cowpox could immunise against smallpox. He made some scratches on the hand of his gardener's eight-year-old son, James Phipps. He rubbed into them some material he had scraped from Sarah's rash. James became ill with cowpox but soon recovered. From this, Jenner knew that cowpox could be passed between human beings. Next he had to prove that having cowpox would protect against smallpox. In July Jenner deliberately infected James with smallpox. To the doctor's delight, James did not catch smallpox. Jenner finally had his proof.

Fact

DIPHTHERIA

In 1883, Theodor Klebs identified the bacterium that caused diphtheria, an acute infection of the throat. In the nineteenth and early twentieth centuries diphtheria was very common and killed 10 per cent of its victims. By 1888 it was found that diphtheria bacteria produce a toxin. In 1891 an antitoxin was discovered but it was not until the 1920s that a reliable vaccine became available. The vaccine was a mixture of toxin and antitoxin, but the toxin had been inactivated, or 'killed', with a formaldehyde solution known as formalin. This principle would later play a major part in the struggle to find a polio vaccine.

much milder. He began to use Hahnemann's methods of following particular cases and making careful recordings of everything he saw.

Jenner noticed that the symptoms of smallpox resembled those of the less dangerous disease cowpox. This affected the udders of cows and was sometimes transferred to humans when they were milking the cows. Cowpox was not life-threatening as smallpox was.

The fact that the two diseases shared similar symptoms set Jenner thinking, and he recorded his observations of people with cowpox. The most significant thing he found was that people who caught cowpox did not seem to catch smallpox. It proved to be a turning point in medical history – Jenner had hit on a way of protecting people from smallpox that was much safer than variolation. He began conducting practical experiments and in 1796 he proved that deliberately infecting someone with cowpox made them immune to smallpox.

Jenner published his results in 1798, but progress was slow. Since no one yet understood how the disease was spread, and standards of hygiene were low, it was easy for the samples of cowpox being used for the

immunisation to become contaminated with real smallpox. As a result, several of Jenner's patients were infected with the deadly disease and some died. This cast doubts upon the process. There was also the problem that doctors who practised variolation were jealous of Jenner's discovery and did not want to lose their trade, which was very lucrative. Jenner was laughed at and his methods were mocked. Cartoons appeared showing people with cows' heads. The doctor knew he had made a great discovery, however, and persisted with his trials. His perseverance paid off and

ABOVE: At first Jenner's vaccine was greeted with contempt, but within a few years people realised its effectiveness and it became compulsory. This engraving, showing working-class people in England queuing to receive the vaccine, was made in 1873.

it was not long before people were forced to admit that Jenner's method of inoculation was much safer than variolation. In 1853, 30 years after his death, Jenner's method was made compulsory by law in England. It was called 'vaccination', from the Latin word for cowpox, *vaccinia*.

NEW RESEARCH INTO DISEASE

Now that the idea of preventing a disease by infecting people with a less-dangerous but similar disease had been proven by Edward Jenner, doctors and scientists started looking for the same solution for other diseases. Many advances were being made in science around this time, and people's understanding of the world around them was improving. One of the most important discoveries was made by the French scientist Louis Pasteur. Pasteur was studying diseases that affected

ABOVE: *This gauge dates from the 1920s and was used to measure the size of smallpox pustules; doctors related the pustules to four different sizes, which indicated what stage the disease was at – the larger the pustules the more progressed the disease.*

RIGHT: *French scientist Louis Pasteur conducting experiments on the fermentation of beer and wine in his laboratory.*

Edité par la CHOCOLATERIE D'AIGUEBELLE (Monastère de la Trappe-Drôme)

PASTEUR DÉCOUVRE LA LOI DES FERMENTS

animals, including anthrax, chicken cholera and rabies. He wondered if there was something in the air that carried the diseases and passed them from one animal to another. To try out his theory, Pasteur conducted experiments with liquids, first storing them in containers that allowed no air in, and then storing them so the liquids were open to the air.

In this way, Pasteur proved that micro-organisms in the air were actually the cause of disease and decay, rather than a by-product of decay. From this time onwards, great advances were made in identifying the different bacteria that caused different diseases. Such discoveries were assisted by the fact that bacteria could now be cultivated and studied through microscopes. Their behaviour could be seen and, most importantly, scientists could see how rapidly bacteria could multiply.

Despite these advances, scientists found that even when all the bacteria and other visible micro-organisms had been filtered out, some diseases and infections still occurred. In 1898 an experiment showed that foot-and-mouth, a disease that affected hoofed animals, could still infect another animal even when everything visible had been filtered out. From this they concluded that there must be something else causing foot-and-mouth and other diseases, which survived the filtration process. Such infections were called filter-passing viruses. It was not until 1937, when the more powerful electron microscope was invented, that they could be seen.

ABOVE: Jenner's work on vaccines opened up a whole new field of research; in the 1920s, an effective vaccine for diphtheria (pictured) was produced. This was a killed-virus vaccine, and influenced the development of the polio vaccine just a few years later.

Key People

Louis Pasteur (1822–95) was a French scientist whose experiments proved to be a turning point in the understanding of how disease is caused. To try to find out what made certain substances decay, he took different liquids – wine, beer and milk – and placed them in special sealed containers so that micro-organisms carried in the air could not get in. The beer and wine did not ferment and the milk did not go off. But when he left the containers open for a few days, allowing the micro-organisms to affect the liquids, the milk went bad and the wine and beer started to ferment. Until Pasteur's work, many scientists had believed the micro-organisms were only produced when substances went rotten. Through Pasteur's experiments, they now knew micro-organisms were around all the time, and could cause disease and decay.

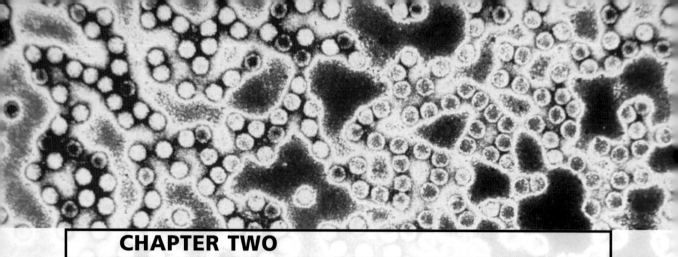

CHAPTER TWO

'There were polio epidemics all the time. You wouldn't go out and play. You wouldn't go to a county fair, wouldn't go to a public swimming location.' **BEN WECHSLER, A PENNSYLVANIA SCHOOLBOY**

The Polio Virus

ABOVE: *This electron microscope image shows a collection of the viruses that cause polio. Polioviruses are very tiny – approximately 25 nanometres (billionths of a metre) in diameter.*

THE DISEASE POLIOMYELITIS HAS BEEN around for many centuries, but in the middle of the nineteenth century, it began to appear in a much more severe form. Previously many people had acquired immunity through weakened strains of the disease that were passed on, for example, through poor sanitation (see p. 18). Now, improved hygiene standards meant that this was not happening, and thousands of children were being permanently crippled in terrible outbreaks. There was widespread panic because no one knew how to prevent or cure the disease.

WHAT IS A VIRUS?

A virus is a micro-organism, made of nucleic acid. It cannot be seen without using a powerful electron microscope. Even the biggest viruses would need 2,000 lined up side by side to measure just 1 mm in length. Viruses are quite different from bacteria, the micro-organisms that cause diseases like typhoid fever and diphtheria. Bacteria are single-celled organisms that can live on their own. They have their own DNA (deoxyribonucleic acid), which contains the genetic instructions for life, allowing them to grow and reproduce without the help of any other organism.

Unlike bacteria, viruses are parasites and cannot live on their own. Viruses do not have their own DNA. Instead they have only RNA (ribonucleic acid). Different types of virus attack different cells – for example, the flu virus attacks cells in the digestive tract, the HIV virus attacks cells in the immune system. However, most types of virus work in the same way. They attach themselves to the cells and then steal resources that their RNA needs to reproduce. This means that the host cell is no longer able to do its own job properly.

Our bodies are equipped to fight off invading bacteria or viruses to a certain degree. Every organism has a unique chemical fingerprint called an antigen. There are millions of white blood cells in the body. Each can recognise an individual antigen and make

BELOW: *How a vaccine works: a weakened form of the virus is injected into the blood. Blood cells in the body create antibodies that kill the weakened virus. If the virus enters the body in the future, the antibodies recognise it and will kill it again.*

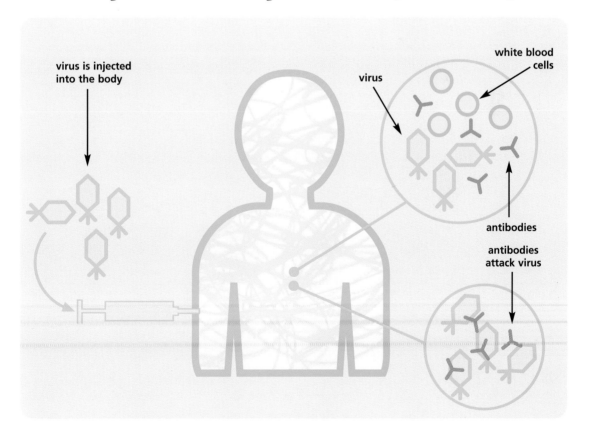

virus is injected into the body

white blood cells

virus

antibodies

antibodies attack virus

antibodies to kill the virus associated with it. They 'remember' the antigen and if that virus ever gets inside the body again, those white blood cells are ready with antibodies. When a person has had a disease and developed antibodies, this is called acquired immunity. Normally it takes several days for white blood cells to make new antibodies to attack a new enemy, and sometimes this does not happen in time to stop a disease from harming the victim. A vaccine uses low doses, which cause the body to make antibodies without allowing it to develop into a dangerous form of the disease. Sometimes 'booster' vaccinations are needed every few years to make sure enough antibodies are still being created.

Fact

BACTERIA AND VIRUSES

Because bacteria and viruses are the two most common causes of disease, people often confuse the two – but they are quite different. Bacteria have all the chemical equipment necessary to reproduce on their own. Viruses have to invade living cells in order to reproduce and cause disease. Bacteria can be treated by a group of drugs known as anti-biotics, which either kill the micro-organisms in the body, or prevent their growth or reproduction. Antibiotics do not work with viruses because viruses are not cells and they do not feed or reproduce like bacteria. When the body's immune system kills a virus, it has to kill the whole cell in which the virus lives.

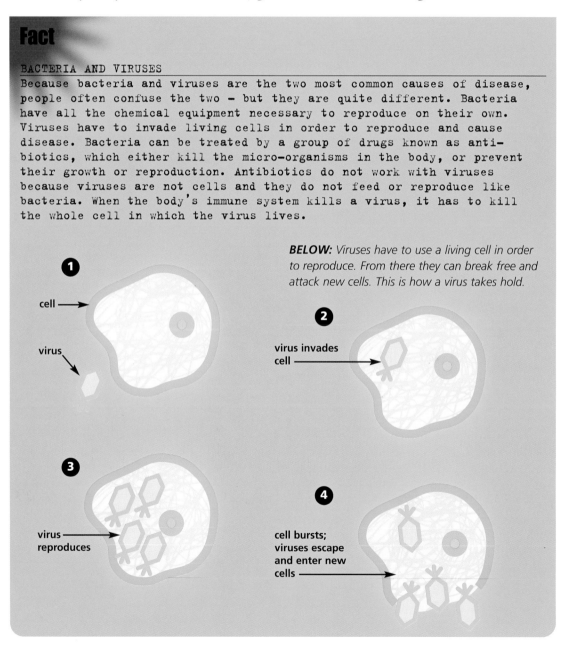

BELOW: *Viruses have to use a living cell in order to reproduce. From there they can break free and attack new cells. This is how a virus takes hold.*

1

cell →

virus

2

virus invades cell →

3

virus → reproduces

4

cell bursts; viruses escape and enter new cells →

Because viruses cannot live on their own, in order to breed them for study and to make vaccines they have to be grown on living tissue. This proved a major problem in developing the polio vaccine.

POLIO – THE DISEASE

Poliomyelitis is very infectious. The virus that causes it, poliovirus, gets into the body through the mouth and finds its way to the intestine, where it reproduces. It is easily passed out of the body in faeces. In this way, in places where sanitation is poor, it can get into the water supply and infect other people.

Many people who catch polio have no symptoms and have no idea they are carrying the disease, or that they are infectious to other people. This makes it very difficult to contain. Sometimes the poliovirus moves out of the intestine and infects the human nervous system. This is where it can do the most harm, by causing paralysis.

ABOVE: *Polio can cause paralysis of the chest muscles and some victims need to be put on an artificial respirator. During the outbreaks in the first half of the twentieth century 'iron lungs' were used. These metal machines were almost the length of a car and exerted a kind of 'push-pull' effect on the sufferer's chest to keep the victim breathing until they recovered and the muscles could function on their own.*

Fact

SYMPTOMS OF POLIO

Polio victims who catch the disease feel fine for a week or two, but then they get a fever and a headache. Most get no worse and soon recover, but for the rest the symptoms start again after a week. Their necks get stiff and the tissue surrounding the brain and spinal cord becomes irritated. If they do not recover within a month, the damage is usually permanent and they are left paralysed.

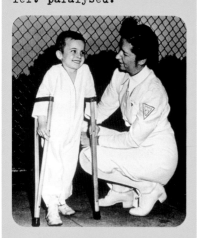

ABOVE: *With the help of crutches and a therapist, this little boy is attempting to build up strength in his legs. Victims of the disease may recover, but often they are left with weakened limbs.*

One in 200 polio victims becomes permanently paralysed, and of these as many as 10 per cent or more may die unless they are put in an artificial respirator, because their chest muscles no longer work well enough for the victim to breathe. There is no cure for polio and it can attack anyone, however old or young they are. Children are more likely to be affected than adults, though.

Although paralysis probably caused by polio was known in ancient Egypt more than 3,000 years ago, at that time – and for many centuries afterwards – the disease rarely caused serious harm. It was so common that babies under six months old often caught polio but were saved by antibodies passed on from their mothers in breast milk, which gave them time to develop their own antibodies to protect them against the disease. Very few of them became ill, but those that did and were paralysed were usually under three years old. Mostly they would be lame in one leg and walk with a limp, or they might have a withered arm where paralysis had caused the muscles to waste.

However, in the nineteenth century polio unexpectedly became a much more serious problem. The first record of an outbreak was in Nottinghamshire, England, in 1835, with another probable outbreak in Louisiana in the USA, in 1841. Reports of polio increased in many countries, especially in Scandinavia. Things soon got much worse. Many people were paralysed, and more seriously so. Dirty streets and open sewers in the cities allowed human faeces carrying poliovirus to contaminate the water supplies. But people did not realise this was what caused the spread of the disease, so polio could break out almost anywhere at any time.

THE POLIO CRISIS

In 1907 polio broke out in New York, affecting more than 2,000 people. In 1916 there was a much more serious outbreak. This time nearly 30,000 people across 20 states caught polio and more than 7,000 died.

Key People

Karl Landsteiner (1868–1943) was one of the first doctors to investigate the possibility of a polio vaccine. In 1909 he gave polio to monkeys by injecting them with tissue taken from a dead human polio victim. In this way he showed that an infectious virus must be the cause of the disease. But early attempts to find a vaccine got nowhere because no one knew there were three different types of poliovirus. Because of this, a vaccine that worked against one type of poliovirus was useless against the other two. In 1931 scientists realised that more than one poliovirus type caused the disease. It took until 1948 to confirm that there were three main types.

In New York alone 9,000 were affected, with 2,500 dying. Almost every summer after this there were serious outbreaks. More older children, teenagers and adults caught the disease.

Why did polio suddenly become so much more widespread, and more severe? It was possibly the result of the way people's everyday lives had changed. By the early twentieth century fewer mothers were breastfeeding their babies, so fewer children were

Fact

PHARAOH SIPTAH
In 1898 the mummy of the Egyptian pharaoh Siptah, who died in 1198 BC, was found. His left leg was withered and shorter than the right one. It seems the pharaoh had suffered from polio in early life and must have walked with very great difficulty.

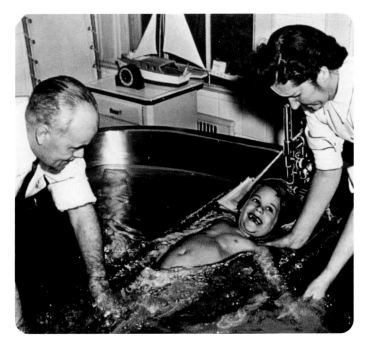

LEFT: A young polio patient smiles as she is immersed in a tub of swirling water as part of her treatment. Doctors tried water therapy to rebuild the muscles that had been wasted by the disease, but many victims remained paralysed.

BELOW: *During the 1916 polio outbreak in New York, people were so afraid of the disease that they fled the city in their thousands.*

receiving the antibodies they needed to fight the disease. Although sanitation levels had improved, polio could still be passed between people where they mixed, especially in swimming pools, where water was easily contaminated; children often had no antibodies to fight the disease, and the older they were the more likely it was that they would be paralysed if they caught it.

Between 1916 and 1934 over 50 per cent of reported polio cases in the world occurred in the United States and Canada, causing widespread terror. The sight of paralysed children and young people horrified the public. Many victims caught polio after being in public places, so hospitals were afraid of caring for those with the disease. Many people panicked and fled from the cities, while con-men started a thriving trade in so-called 'miracle cures'.

Fact

THE INFLUENZA EPIDEMIC

In 1918 a severe form of influenza broke out. In the USA and Europe, four years of food rationing because of the war had resulted in poor diets that reduced the effectiveness of the immune system and made people more susceptible to influenza. The virus spread worldwide and killed millions. In the USA 25 million people caught it, and around 550,000 died. Until HIV/AIDS became widespread in the 1980s, this was the worst epidemic in history.

RIGHT: The blocks here show tissue samples from victims of the influenza epidemic of 1918. They are lying on a list of those who died.

After the 1916 epidemic, the US Public Health Service realised that most of the New York population had probably caught polio, but because they did not become ill, they had no idea they were carrying the disease and could be spreading it. This meant that measures like putting victims in quarantine would not work – there were simply too many people who were likely to be carrying the disease. Only a vaccine could protect everyone.

In 1934 public fundraising began to help finance the search for a vaccine. Over $1 million was raised immediately. However, even though the problem of financing was being addressed, there were other, scientific issues that needed to be resolved. Most importantly, no one knew how to measure poliovirus or the antibodies it produced, and until they could do this, working out the correct dosage of

THE MARCH OF DIMES
The US campaign to raise
money for polio research
was known as 'The March
of Dimes', because it
was suggested that
people showed their
support by sending their
dimes (ten-cent pieces)
direct to the president.
In 1938 $268,000 in
dimes was sent to the
National Foundation
for Infantile Paralysis.
$1.8 million was raised
that year in total.
In 1955 nearly $67
million was spent on
care for polio patients,
information, education
and further research
into the disease.

RIGHT: *Prince Rainier III of Monaco and his wife, the actress Grace Kelly, gave support to the fundraising, which became known as the March of Dimes.*

the vaccine was pretty much impossible. Also, medical scientists still could not tell one type of poliovirus from another.

These facts did not prevent some scientists from rushing ahead and giving vaccines to children, even though they had not been properly tested. Dr John Kolmer, from the Temple University Medical School in Pennsylvania, created a vaccine from a poliovirus that he believed he had made harmless. He vaccinated 12,000 children against this virus before testing it properly and observing the results. Tragically, six of the children died and three were paralysed. Such disasters made other scientists believe there was little chance of a reliable polio vaccine ever being made.

THE NATIONAL FOUNDATION FOR INFANTILE PARALYSIS

In 1938 US President Franklin D. Roosevelt established the National Foundation for Infantile Paralysis (NFIP). The president suffered from paralysis that, at the time, was believed to have been caused by polio. He caught the disease in 1921, when he was nearly 40 years old. He wore steel braces on his legs and found it very difficult to walk, so he spent much of his time in a wheelchair. Although he played down his disability in public, he used his position as president to promote research into the disease and before he founded the NFIP, he organised and hosted many events to raise money. In 2003, researchers suggested that Roosevelt may not have had polio after all, but instead may have suffered from a disease called Guillain-Barré Syndrome, which causes the immune system to attack healthy tissue, resulting in many symptoms similar to those of polio. We may never know the truth – and it would not have made much difference to the president, as there were no good treatments for either disease at the time. Today the cause of Guillain-Barré Syndrome is still unknown. Most patients now recover from the disease, but they may need to spend months being cared for in intensive-care units in hospitals, and they may end up wheelchair-bound.

Roosevelt's National Foundation was a great success, and was supported by public donations, which became known as 'The March of Dimes'. The organisation set out to find a researcher who could develop a vaccine for them. That man was Jonas Salk.

ABOVE: *US president Franklin D. Roosevelt in 1928, walking with the help of crutches. He established the National Foundation for Infantile Paralysis in 1938 to raise money for research into a vaccine.*

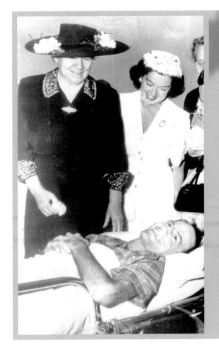

Key People

Sister Elizabeth Kenny (1880–1952, pictured on the left) was an Australian nurse who became well-known in the 1930s and 1940s for her treatment of polio victims. People who had been paralysed by polio were usually placed in plaster in the belief it would stop their limbs becoming deformed. Heavy leg-irons and braces were also used, which seriously limited movement and recovery. Sister Kenny believed treatment with moist hot-packs on muscles could help patients recover the use of their limbs when combined with exercise and retraining of muscle movement. At a time when there was still no vaccine, she had considerable success and became famous in Australia, Britain and the USA. Her love of publicity and lack of scientific expertise meant she was unpopular with some doctors. However, her instinctive knowledge made a real difference to the lives of many polio victims.

CHAPTER THREE

'It is courage based on confidence, not daring, and it is confidence based on experience.'

JONAS SALK, ON TRYING THE EXPERIMENTAL VACCINE ON HIMSELF AND HIS FAMILY

Salk's Investigations

DR JONAS SALK HAD A SPECIAL INTEREST IN VACCINES, AND WAS undertaking research at the University of Michigan with a team led by Dr Thomas Francis. Under Francis, Salk helped search for an influenza vaccine. He succeeded in developing one that was used in the Second World War. The research programme's patron was the US Army, which feared an outbreak of influenza as serious as that of 1918–19. Salk's work was vital in the development of vaccines to control viruses. In 1947 he was hired by the University of Pittsburgh's School of Medicine to continue his work on influenza. It was one of those lucky chances in medical history.

ABOVE: *Dr Jonas Salk (right), during experiments to find a vaccine that would be effective against the three types of poliovirus.*

SALK'S SOLUTIONS

Harry Weaver, a leading member of the National Foundation for Infantile Paralysis, paid a visit to Salk at Pittsburgh, and asked him to head the polio vaccine research funded by the president's organisation. Salk was delighted at being offered the opportunity. The search for a polio vaccine was a national campaign with a very high profile – he would have the money and resources to hire the right team and to do something important that would be recognised not only across America, but also, perhaps, in the many

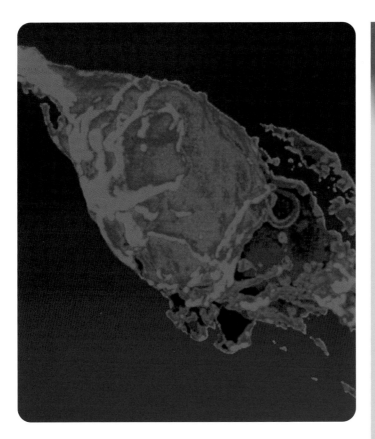

ABOVE: *This microscopic image (magnified 9,000 times) shows a cell infected with poliovirus. The red patches to the centre right are the poliovirus micro-organisms attacking the surface of the cell.*

Fact

TYPES OF POLIOVIRUS

One of the major problems scientists found in creating a polio vaccine was that there are three different types of poliovirus, and vaccinating against one did not prevent a person getting a different type. Today, all three types are included in the vaccine.

TYPE I: this is the type that most often caused epidemics; it frequently resulted in paralysis of the legs, arms and breathing muscles.

TYPE II: this was least likely to cause paralysis, but could result in severe damage to the brain stem.

TYPE III: this was the most rare but also the most dangerous; it caused leg and arm paralysis as well as damaging the brain stem.

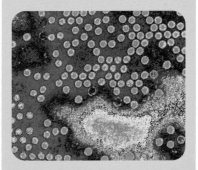

ABOVE: *A poliovirus (green) belonging to Type I. Type I is the virus that causes most epidemics and often results in paralysis.*

other countries – particularly across Europe – that were suffering the effects of poliomyelitis.

By the time Salk had set up the research team and started work on a polio vaccine, there was more urgency than ever. Polio was causing outbreaks almost every year, and people were growing more and more afraid of this terrible disease.

Scientists already knew that 125 individual forms of polioviruses existed. The symptoms of the disease led them to belive that these could be divided into three 'types' – numbered I, II and III (see Fact box). In order to be completely effective, they had to create a vaccine that would work against all three, otherwise the patient would be protected against one, but could easily catch another type. Salk had to know which type every one of the 125 viruses belonged to. This was

Fact

going to be a long job, as the established process of testing was slow and expensive. He began to think that there must be a better way.

Salk's solution was brilliant. He realised that although some polioviruses are much weaker than others, they all encourage the body to make similar numbers of antibodies. He gave a poliovirus of an unknown type to a monkey. The monkey developed antibodies, which Salk then tested against polioviruses of a known type. If the monkey's antibodies killed a Type I virus, then the unknown virus must be Type I too. If not he knew it must be Type II or Type III, so he tried the antibodies against a Type II poliovirus. If they killed the virus then he knew the unknown virus was Type II. If not, then it must be Type III. Salk was criticised for changing the established methods of researching the vaccine – people preferred tried-and-proved methods when it came to medical research – but Salk knew the need was desperate and that his methods were much faster.

THE PACE OF RESEARCH QUICKENS

Two other polio researchers, working independently, helped Salk look for a safe vaccine. In 1948 Dr Isabel Morgan of Baltimore in the USA was working with killed-virus vaccines that would stop monkeys from being infected. She killed the poliovirus with formalin, thus creating polio antibodies in monkeys

Key People

Jonas Salk (1914–95) had planned to study law, but while at the City College of New York he grew interested in biology and chemistry, especially the study of diseases. He went on to study at the New York University School of Medicine. Salk was interested in whether viruses such as influenza and polio could be made harmless but still be effective as a vaccine. He was convinced it would work, even though at the time nobody else believed it would. It turned out he was right, and the method became known as the 'inactive' or 'killed' virus.

without infecting them. She found that she could only grow the poliovirus antibodies in nervous tissue from the spinal cords of monkeys. It would not be beneficial for humans because in previous research it had been found that humans are highly allergic to nervous tissue from other animals. However, this was still a step in the right direction.

Around the same time, another great breakthrough was made by an independent team. The scientist John F. Enders, working in Boston, reported that he had successfully grown poliovirus in a test-tube containing non-nervous tissue. The new antibiotic drug penicillin was now available for treating bacterial infection. Penicillin was used to kill those annoying bacteria that had previously prevented researchers from growing viruses on little scraps of living tissue. Salk and his team could now grow as much poliovirus as they needed to study it properly.

ABOVE: *John F. Enders (right) and Dr Thomas Weller examine poliovirus in a tissue culture at their research laboratory in Boston in 1954. Enders' experiments in growing polioviruses on non-nervous tissue meant that Salk and his team could grow as much as they needed for their own investigations.*

Fact

THE PRESSURE TO FIND A VACCINE
In 1952 there was a serious polio
outbreak in Copenhagen, Denmark and
another in the USA, where nearly
58,000 cases were reported and more
than 3,000 people died. Once again,
the nations affected were thrown
into panic on a huge scale. Children
were kept away from public places
and even schools, as parents feared
the infection would strike their
families without warning. People
were even afraid of visiting each
others' houses for fear of catching
the disease. Such a disaster did
have a positive effect, however.
There was an outcry for a vaccine
and donations poured in from the
public. In the USA, the country
leading the research, the government
did not struggle to find funding —
so serious was the situation that
everybody was willing to help.

ABOVE: *A man in an iron lung in an ambulance in the early 1950s. The mirror on the iron lung allowed the patient to see at least a little of what was going on around him or her.*

THE SUCCESS OF THE MONKEY TRIALS

Salk's research team was divided into groups, each working on a specific task. One team was charged with finding the monkey tissue on which polio grew best; another team worked on making poliovirus inactive but still effective enough that antibodies were produced when it was injected into laboratory animals.

In 1951 they began to experiment by injecting monkeys with poliovirus. Until Salk's work, many scientists thought that only live vaccines worked. Salk believed that an inactive virus vaccine would be just as good and probably safer. He knew that formalin was already being used to make an inactive virus vaccine to treat diphtheria, and thought that this might work on his own vaccine. So Salk's team used formalin to inactivate the poliovirus. They discovered that tissue taken from monkeys' kidneys was the best for growing the virus from which the vaccine could be made.

Salk and his team were moving on apace, but there were still many issues to be addressed. It was vital to find out exactly how much formalin to use. Too much could damage the virus in the vaccine so much that no antibodies would be produced when it was given to patients. Too little, and the vaccine might give the patient full-blown polio before there was time for antibodies to be made.

In 1952 Salk's researchers hit on the right amount of formalin to make a vaccine against all three types of poliovirus. It created a vaccine that was strong enough to

Key People

Dr Hilary Koprowski (b. 1916) was an industrial researcher and one of the pioneers of the polio vaccine. He began his research in 1947. Although Salk was still testing his vaccine on monkeys, Koprowski went one step further. In 1950 he conducted an unofficial experiment. He used a weakened Type II poliovirus to experiment on children. His experiment worked: the children developed antibodies and none got polio. Thanks to Koprowski, Salk knew that a vaccine which worked on monkeys should also work on humans.

encourage the production of antibodies against all forms of polio, but was too weak to be dangerous. It was called 'inactive' polio vaccine, known as IPV. The team spent a year trying it out on monkeys. In order to be effective the vaccine had to be given on two occasions, one month apart, and they estimated that boosters would be needed after five years to maintain immunity.

While Salk and his team worked frantically to satisfy the public demand for a successful vaccine, the panic continued across Europe and the USA. Salk knew they had to come up with something soon. His luck held out. Trials showed that the IPV worked. The monkeys did not catch polio from the vaccine. After 21 days they had developed sufficient antibodies of their own, so that they did not catch polio even when they were deliberately infected. The next stage was to try it out on humans.

BACKGROUND: *A young girl turns away as Salk – helped by a nurse – gives a dose of his vaccine during the trials he began in 1952.*

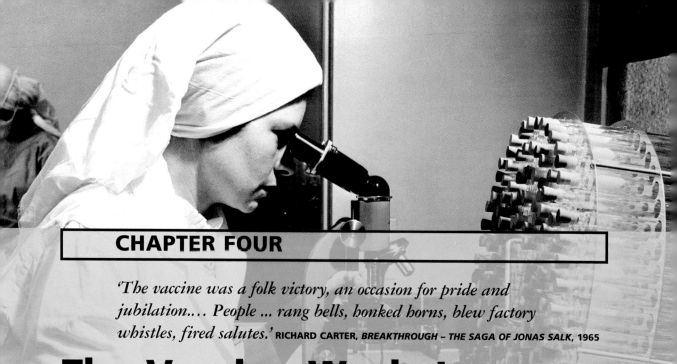

CHAPTER FOUR

'The vaccine was a folk victory, an occasion for pride and jubilation.... People ... rang bells, honked horns, blew factory whistles, fired salutes.' RICHARD CARTER, *BREAKTHROUGH – THE SAGA OF JONAS SALK*, 1965

The Vaccine Works!
Field Tests and Mass Trials

ABOVE: *A technician inspects samples of the vaccine at a laboratory in California, during the mass trials that took place throughout 1954.*

TESTING A NEW VACCINE IS RISKY. IF IT goes wrong the vaccine can cause the disease it was supposed to prevent. But the polio vaccine had to be tested on people. Salk decided to try out his vaccine on patients who had already had polio, as he knew they could not catch it again.

HUMAN TRIALS BEGIN

Salk started secret trials at a home for polio victims in Leetsdale, Pennsylvania, in June 1952. He took blood samples from 45 children who had had polio and also from 27 staff members who had not had the disease. He wanted to see if the vaccine would raise antibody levels in both groups.

Salk found that the polio vaccine 'boosted' the antibody levels in the children, and gave the staff members the same level of antibodies as they would have had following natural infection. The blood samples from the vaccinated people were placed on tissue cultures of poliovirus. Antibodies in the blood killed the virus. The early signs were promising.

However many volunteers Salk had used, it still was not enough. Trials of any new vaccine have to be as extensive as possible to give the greatest chance of finding side-effects. But excitement grew when Salk published his early results, and permission for mass trials was granted.

The mass trials started in the spring of 1954. The vaccine was to be tried out in 217 areas in 44 American states, with around 30,000 medical staff and others involved in managing the project. Around 1.8 million schoolchildren, aged between six and nine, were given the vaccine. The programme was one of the first in history to be recorded on computers. It was vital that every child's progress was monitored accurately.

A BAD BATCH

On 12 April 1955 Salk publicly announced that the vaccine was effective. It was ten years to the day since Franklin D. Roosevelt had died. Salk became a national hero, something he feared, as he believed he would become known as a 'glory hound'. Some of his medical rivals were jealous, especially as journalists called his discovery the 'Salk vaccine'. People said that he had depended on the work of a lot of other people, which was now going unacknowledged, in a quest for personal glory.

LEFT: *Just minutes after the success of the Salk vaccine was announced in 1955, cases of the vaccine were loaded on to planes in Philadelphia, where it was manufactured by the drug company Wyeth, and distributed around the USA.*

Fact

MASS VACCINATIONS
By August 1955 more than four million vaccinations had been given. In the same year there were around 30,000 cases of polio in the United States. In 1956 it was half that, and by 1957 there were just 6,000 cases.

ABOVE: By the time Salk announced the success in 1955, there was never a greater need for it. This hospital ward in Boston shows why: many people were living in iron lungs to help them breathe, and cases of polio in the USA were still widespread.

RIGHT: Samples of Salk's first vaccine, from 1955. This box contains three vials of the vaccine.

The general public did not care. They were ecstatic – the disease that had cast a shadow of fear over their lives for so long – a disease that crippled children and young people – now looked as if it could be controlled. Word spread, and Salk's polio vaccine was rapidly introduced in other countries.

But there was a nasty shock in store. During the mass trials there had been concerns that a live virus might get into the vaccine. Later the same month, news broke that some vaccinated children had caught polio. People were devastated. If this was true, it would destroy the whole principle of Salk's inactive-virus vaccine. Immunisation was immediately suspended and investigations into the new cases of polio were ordered.

The cases were traced back to a bad batch of vaccine – made by a company called Cutter – that still contained live poliovirus. Around 260 cases of polio were caused in 25 states, and 11 people died. Idaho was one of the worst affected: 25 children caught polio from the vaccine and passed it on to 61 other people. Of the 86 involved in the Idaho outbreak, 70 were paralysed.

Some experts wanted immunisation stopped permanently. It was obvious that vaccine batches were not being tested properly; but it was also clear that there would always be some risk that live viruses could end up in vaccines. Salk helped to tighten up production standards. Immunisations resumed, but Salk's opponents had the proof they wanted that an inactive vaccine was potentially unreliable. Some of the public still feared children would catch polio from the vaccine. In New York, up to 30 per cent of children did not turn up for their jabs.

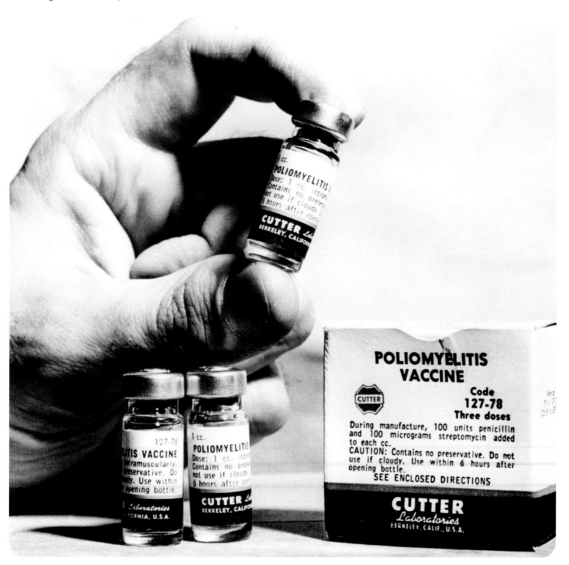

CHAPTER FIVE

'The Salk Vaccine is Safe, Effective, and Potent. Polio is Conquered.'

US NEWSPAPER HEADLINE, 12 APRIL 1955

New Vaccines

ABOVE: *In 1955, thousands of schoolchildren, like these in San Diego, California, were administered the vaccine as part of a mass-inoculation programme.*

RIGHT: *Between 1916 and 1934 over half of the cases of polio worldwide were reported in the USA and Canada. After the outbreak in 1916 (occurring mainly in New York), cases of polio declined and then levelled off, although the disease was still very much in evidence. The epidemic reached its peak in 1952, but with the introduction of the vaccine, cases dropped dramatically and by 1965 there were only 61 new cases reported in the USA.*

SALK'S NEW POLIO VACCINE WAS A massive breakthrough, but it was far from perfect. The public had believed the vaccine was 100 per cent effective, but it was not. In reality it was only around 90 per cent effective. After the Cutter incident, some people believed it was unsafe. It was expensive and difficult to make, and time-consuming and costly to vaccinate large numbers of people because it needed two injections and boosters every five years for life.

SABIN VS SALK

Dr Albert Sabin was working on a different polio vaccine. He believed Salk's vaccine would never work. Even when it was proved to be effective, Sabin attacked Salk in newspaper articles and interviews. It was partly because of this rivalry that the Enders team won the 1954 Nobel Prize for Medicine instead of Salk (for their discovery that viruses could be grown on ordinary living tissue without fear of contamination). Salk was still being criticised by other scientists.

Key People

Albert Sabin (1906–93) spent a lifetime researching vaccines and viral diseases, including polio. From 1939 he worked at the University of Cincinnati College of Medicine. Sabin was one of the first to realise that, by this time, polio had actually become rare in cities where sanitation was poor; this meant that children had probably acquired the antibodies needed through a weakened strain of the virus, which would have been transferred through poor sanitation systems. He also believed that babies must have acquired immunity from their mothers. He was strongly opposed to Salk's method of using a killed-virus vaccine, and invented an oral vaccination using the live virus.

Of course, Salk's work had been far more difficult than some critics said, but Sabin and others believed that an inactive-virus vaccine simply was not strong enough to give long-term protection. They had some good reasons for thinking this. An inactive-virus vaccine for mumps had been developed in the United States in 1948. It worked, but not very well. People vaccinated with it only stayed immune for around a year.

Meanwhile, polio outbreaks continued to appear, especially in Canada. Antibodies produced by Salk's vaccine only stopped polioviruses from getting into the nervous system. A person vaccinated this way would usually not develop full-blown polio, but might still be carrying it in his or her intestine, and could pass the disease on to other people. It seemed that Salk's vaccine could not stop polio spreading.

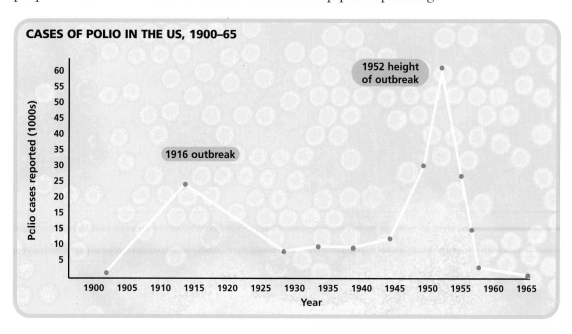

CASES OF POLIO IN THE US, 1900–65

BELOW: People in America queued in their thousands to receive their polio vaccinations at dedicated sites in every town and city. The result of this was that by 1960, only 2,500 new cases of polio were reported in the USA (in 1952, there had been nearly 58,000 cases). This picture shows an immunisation centre in Texas in 1962.

Fact

THE VACCINE'S SUCCESS

The introduction of the Salk and Sabin vaccines had a dramatic effect on polio in the USA. In 1955 nearly 29,000 cases were reported, but in 1960 there were around 2,500 cases. By 1965 there were just 61. Since then there have been fewer than 10 per year, usually caused by the vaccine itself. In 1994 it was announced that polio had been eradicated in North America.

ABOVE: Jonas Salk receiving an award from US president Eisenhower, to acknowledge his contribution to the decline of polio.

SABIN'S VACCINE

Sabin believed the vaccine had to behave as much as possible like the real disease, so that polioviruses were fought throughout the body, including the intestine. He was convinced that his polio vaccine would be cheaper, easier to use and more effective.

Sabin isolated weak versions of each of the three main poliovirus types, growing the viruses on the kidney cells of monkeys. These viruses would infect human beings, but not seriously. They would invade the digestive system and grow there but, unlike the dangerous forms of polio, they stayed put and did not infect the nervous system. The virus remains in the body and encourages the continued production of antibodies, making immunity long-term. Even when weakened it can pass to non-vaccinated people, who then make their own antibodies and become immune too.

Sabin's vaccine could be swallowed on a lump of sugar or taken in a spoonful of syrup. That made it far cheaper, so governments and doctors liked it, and much easier to give to children, which meant parents and children liked it too. It was called an oral polio vaccine, or OPV.

Trials of Sabin's new vaccine started in 1957 in the Netherlands, Sweden, the Soviet Union, Mexico, Chile and Japan. It had to be given to a child three times in the first two years of life, followed by a booster when the child started school. There was no need for further vaccinations.

Even this was not perfect, though. Being 'live', Sabin's vaccine can mutate back into a dangerous form. Approximately one in 3.5 million people catch polio from the Sabin vaccine today. By 1964 at least 57 cases of polio leading to paralysis had been caused by the Sabin vaccine in the USA. Also, Sabin's vaccine could not be used on anyone who was already weak or ill. Even though the virus was weakened it could give such people full-blown polio. This meant that anyone working with those sick people, such as doctors or nurses, could not use it either, in case their patients caught polio from them. In the developing world especially, other viruses in the gut can stop the polio vaccine from encouraging antibody production. These problems highlighted the fact that, even after all the research, poliovirus was still not fully understood. Despite the difficulties, Sabin's vaccine was cheaper, easier to take and usually more effective than Salk's. By 1962 it was licensed in the USA.

Fact

NEW VACCINATIONS

Now that it was possible to grow viruses in bulk, research could expand in ways previously thought impossible. Polio became part of the series of routine immunisations that included DTP, already being given for diphtheria, whooping cough ('pertussis') and tetanus, licensed in 1958. The Enders team had shown how viruses could be grown on ordinary living tissue without fear of contamination. In 1954 Enders isolated the measles virus. A measles vaccine was developed by 1960, but it was not made available for the public until 1964. A rubella vaccine was licensed in 1969. The last major epidemic of rubella in the USA was in 1964, causing damage to 20,000 unborn babies. By 1972 the combined measles–mumps–rubella vaccine, known as MMR, had become available. It vaccinates against all three diseases in one dose.

ABOVE: These are bottles of the MMR (measles-mumps rubella) vaccine. Like the polio vaccine, at first this was hailed as a breakthrough, but recently some doctors have suggested that this combined vaccine might have serious side-effects.

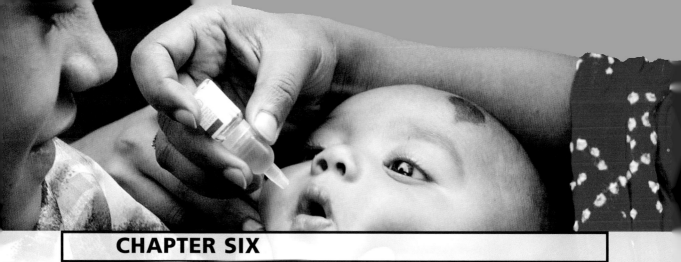

CHAPTER SIX

'The goal of the Global Polio Eradication Initiative is to ensure that no child will ever again know the crippling effects of polio.'
WORLD HEALTH ORGANIZATION

Polio Today

ABOVE: *The oral vaccine in India.*

BELOW: *Kits like this are used in vaccination programmes all over the world. The inoculation gun forces the vaccine through the skin without the use of a needle, and makes mass vaccination much more efficient.*

THE SALK AND SABIN POLIO VACCINES showed how difficult it was to develop effective vaccines, because the disease can still fight back. Even in countries where vaccination is well-established, diseases can still break out, proving that micro-organisms are all around us and can mutate into new forms that are unaffected by vaccines. Both the Salk and Sabin vaccines have the potential to cause the disease they are designed to prevent.

THE DECLINE OF POLIO IN THE WEST

In 1959 the English footballer Jeff Hall was killed by polio. The high profile of this case reminded people of the dangers of the disease and encouraged them to have the vaccination. However, the subsequent reduction in polio cases made them believe they were safe and that polio would soon be eradicated. Vaccination numbers dropped once again. This fluctuation was reflected in countries across Europe, but government initiatives in the following decades made people realise that if there

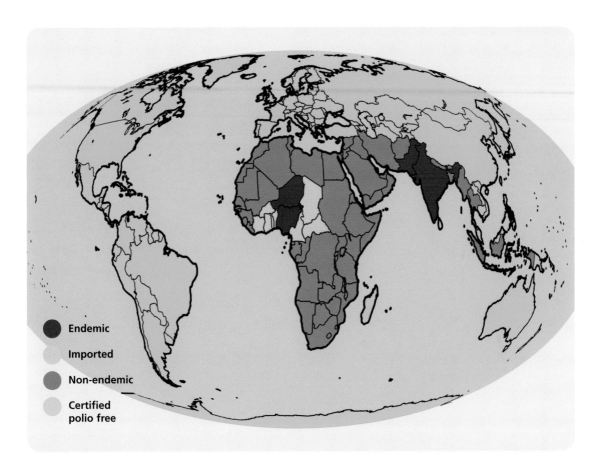

Endemic

Imported

Non-endemic

Certified
polio free

was any hope of eradicating polio, everyone must take the vaccine, and the situation improved. The last cases of polio in the USA were recorded in 1979 and shortly afterwards in Europe. However, it remained endemic in 125 countries across the world. India and some African countries were among the worst affected.

ABOVE: Polio cases worldwide today. Europe and the US are polio-free. However, polio is still endemic (present in a specific, localised area) in a few parts of Africa and India, and in other countries, while not endemic, cases are still found.

NEW OUTBREAKS OF POLIO

In 1988, 350,000 cases of polio were reported in the developing world and 116,000 in 1990, but it is almost impossible to get accurate figures. In remote farming areas polio cases can be completely missed by official records. The vaccine can still mutate and cause outbreaks of polio, especially where the numbers of the population being vaccinated fall below 90 per cent. Polio broke out in the Dominican Republic in 1999 and Haiti in 2001 because less than 80 per cent of the population had been vaccinated. In China in 2000 a

Fact

THE SALK AND SABIN VACCINES TODAY
Until about 2000, Sabin's vaccine was the one most commonly used around the world. However, because it is a live-virus vaccine, it still causes about seven cases of polio a year in countries where it is used. This has incited medical scientists to look again at the advantages and disadvantages of both types of vaccine, and Salk's killed-virus vaccine is now more common once again.

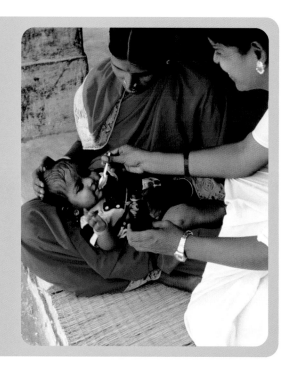

RIGHT: *A baby is given Sabin's oral vaccine in India. Until recently, this was the preferred method, but because it causes polio in a very small number of cases, some experts now feel that Salk's vaccine is better after all.*

mass-vaccination programme followed an outbreak in Qinghai province. In 2002 cases of polio were still occurring in Africa, the Middle East, India and South-East Asia. By the end of 2003 it was only endemic in parts of Nigeria, Pakistan and India.

Today people travel around the world routinely. Anyone carrying the disease can quite easily introduce it to another country, or someone could catch it while in another country. In areas of low vaccination rates, a polio outbreak can spread rapidly amongst non-vaccinated children with no natural immunity. So it remains important to maintain immunity levels everywhere.

In western Uttar Pradesh in India there have been recent cases of polio. Poliovirus exports pose an ever-present threat, particularly in West Africa. In 2003, a polio outbreak in Nigeria spread to neighbouring polio-free countries. Children in these countries are particularly vulnerable, as a lack of funds has resulted in a stop to immunisation campaigns, leaving millions at risk of being infected. In March 2004 another serious issue arose when a large batch of polio vaccine was found to be contaminated, and in the public scare that followed, thousands of people refused to be vaccinated. The problems, it seems, are not over.

PLANS FOR A POLIO-FREE WORLD

The official campaign to wipe out polio was launched in 1985. Eradicating the disease means immunising all children with four doses in their first year. National Immunisation Days mean that a very large number of children can be vaccinated at once. In Brazil in 1980 320,000 volunteers at 90 centres treated 20 million children. This schedule has since been maintained. In some countries 'door-to-door' campaigns have to be arranged to reach children who have been missed out. Finally, every case of paralysis in children has to be investigated immediately to see whether polio was the cause. That can help to stop local epidemics.

Fears remain, however, that polio could turn up by accident or malicious design. Poliovirus stocks in laboratories or vaccine-production factories could escape if a staff member became infected and did not realise. It is also possible that terrorists could try to steal the virus or even isolate forms of poliovirus.

Fact

MUTATING VIRUSES
For the moment polio vaccines are effective against the three known virus types that cause it. But the influenza virus mutates continually, so new influenza vaccines have to be developed all the time. HIV/AIDS is caused by a virus that destroys the body's immune system. It mutates continuously and so quickly that it has so far proved impossible to make a vaccine. It is not unlikely that poliovirus could also mutate into a form that is not affected by the vaccine.

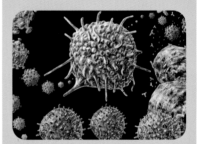

ABOVE: The HIV virus that causes AIDS is a mutating virus, so developing a vaccine is very difficult. The virus particles (the green-and-brown spheres left and top right) attack white blood cells, and the antibodies are unable to kill them.

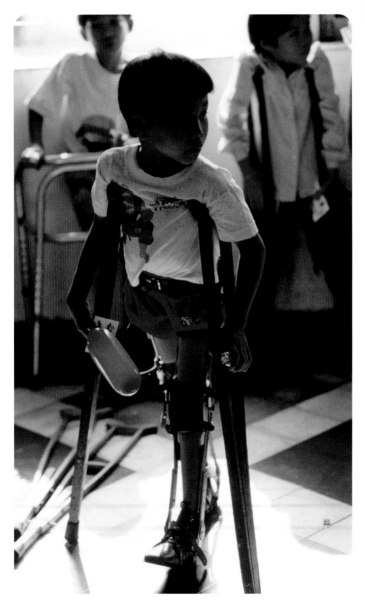

LEFT: This Vietnamese boy lives in an orphanage for children affected by polio. Even in countries where the disease is no longer widespread, those who suffered during the outbreaks in the 1950s and before are still living with the effects of the disease.

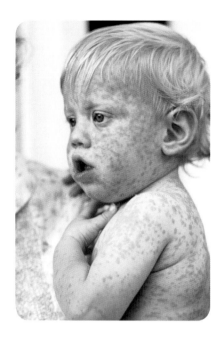

ABOVE: *This young child has measles – it can be dangerous and most people have their children vaccinated as babies to prevent the disease.*

In 2002 Dr Eckard Wimmer's research team at the University of New York announced they had created an artificial poliovirus using polio's genetic code, proving viruses could be made by bioterrorists.

LIVING WITH THE EFFECTS OF POLIO

Today there are an estimated 20 million people worldwide who suffered from polio at its height in the 1940s and 1950s. At the time, they faced years in hospital before they could recover some mobility. Many of these people are still suffering from the after-effects of this vicious disease. Doctors are discovering late-onset effects even in people who seem to have made a full recovery. These include muscle weakness, having problems breathing or swallowing, muscle pain and unusual tiredness. This is called 'post-polio syndrome' and it proves the one significant problem with the vaccine – it can prevent polio, but it cannot cure it.

OTHER VIRUSES AND VACCINES

The battle against diseases takes a very long time. Even in the twentieth century, smallpox was killing millions of people. In 1967 the World Health Organization (WHO) announced a programme to wipe out smallpox from the world. Success depended on organisation, money and worldwide acceptance of vaccination. For a disease to be eradicated, at least 80 per cent (preferably 90 per cent) of the population has to be immunised, to stop the disease circulating. When fewer people are vaccinated, the disease can still be caught and passed on to others. But achieving 90 per cent immunisation means organising routine vaccinations so that everyone is reached. In developed countries children are routinely vaccinated. In a country where vaccination is new, a programme to vaccinate everyone in a short space of time is required, followed by routine vaccination of children and babies. Nearly 200 years after Edward Jenner's work with cowpox, it was announced in 1980 that smallpox had finally been eradicated.

Fact

THE DIPHTHERIA VACCINE
By the 1920s a vaccine was available for diphtheria, a disease that was more common than polio and had a higher death rate. But many people distrusted the idea of being vaccinated at all. The diphtheria vaccine was tried out in Britain. Only when news of its success spread was it gradually adopted, with mass vaccinations beginning in 1941. By the early 1950s diphtheria had almost disappeared.

The successful measles-mumps-rubella vaccination (MMR) has become a major issue in several developed countries. In the 1990s some parents reported that their children developed intestinal diseases and autism after receiving the MMR vaccination. Some believe that giving three vaccinations at once is the problem. Almost all doctors and medical researchers say there is no evidence that MMR vaccinations cause autism. But popular fear has meant that in the United Kingdom, and especially in London, vaccination levels have fallen so far that there is a risk of a measles epidemic. Some parents have paid to have their children vaccinated against each disease separately. Today, research into the possible link is being carried out in the USA.

ABOVE: *Immunisation is the most effective way of preventing disease. The fact that we are now on the verge of eliminating polio entirely is a testimony to this.*

WHAT DOES THE FUTURE HOLD?

With the eradication of polio, it will be possible to end vaccination programmes. Tremendous progress has been made in the global fight against polio since 1985, when the World Health Organization resolved to eradicate the disease. Today, the world has its best chance to stop the transmission of poliovirus. There were just 700 cases reported worldwide in 2003 and WHO announced that the disease would have disappeared by 2005. For the first time, this is a real possibility.

RIGHT: *A dose of Sabin's live vaccine, still used today. It is given orally in three doses at intervals of not less than one month.*

'Never before has commitment and effort been so focused on this final push to rid the world of polio. Not only is the world on the verge of reaching a global health goal – the eradication of polio will also leave behind a legacy of what can be achieved through an extraordinary demonstration of global cooperation.'
THE WORLD HEALTH ORGANIZATION, 2004

TIMELINE

1718	Lady Mary Wortley Montagu introduces variolation to England from Turkey
1835	Worksop, Nottinghamshire, sees the first modern report of a polio epidemic
1853	Jenner's vaccination against smallpox is made compulsory in England
1909	Dr Karl Landsteiner discovers that polio is caused by a virus-borne infection
1916	First major outbreak of polio in the USA
1931	Scientists discover that polio is caused by more than one type of virus
1938	Roosevelt creates the National Foundation for Infantile Paralysis
1947	Salk is appointed to run the polio vaccine research programme at the University of Pittsburgh; Britain suffers its first major polio outbreak – nearly 8,000 cases are reported
1948	Dr Isabel Morgan pioneers the use of the 'killed' virus, grown in monkey neural tissue, to immunise monkeys
1949	Dr John F. Enders pioneers the process of growing poliovirus in non-neural tissue cultures
1950	Salk uses the Enders technique to grow a virus
1951	Salk's team uses formalin to kill the virus they have grown, experimenting on monkeys successfully to produce immunity
1952	Major polio outbreaks in Denmark and the USA – nearly 58,000 US cases of polio are reported; trials of the vaccine begin in Pennsylvania
1954	Mass trials begin; in April
1955	Salk announces the success of the vaccine; Albert Sabin begins work on a live-virus vaccine
1961	Polio is reduced in the US by 95 per cent; in Britain, an outbreak in Hull proves that polio still poses a threat
1962	Sabin's live-virus vaccine is introduced
1988	The World Health Assembly votes for a global polio eradication programme; 350,000 cases of polio are reported worldwide
1999	Sabin's vaccine is discontinued in the USA to prevent further outbreaks
2003	Fewer than 700 cases are reported worldwide; the World Health Organization announces that the world will be free of polio by 2005
2004	A bad batch of polio vaccine is found in Nigeria, resulting in a public scare and many people refusing to be vaccinated; the British government revives the safer killed-virus vaccine for a new multi-vaccine

GLOSSARY

AIDS Acquired Immuno Deficiency Syndrome; a disease that destroys the human immune system, allowing other diseases that would not normally kill to take over unchecked.

ALCHEMY A medieval science that sought to turn base metals into gold and to search for an 'elixir' that would prolong human life.

ANTIBODY Produced by white blood cells to attack invaders in the body such as bacteria or viruses.

ANTIGEN A protein produced by all living matter, serving as a kind of chemical fingerprint. White blood cells recognise antigens on bacteria and viruses, and produce antibodies to inactivate them.

ANTITOXIN An antibody that can destroy a certain toxin in the human body.

AUTISM A condition of the brain where a person can see and hear, but has difficulty with communication and social interaction.

BACTERIUM A single-celled micro-organism capable of independent life. Only some bacteria cause disease.

BOOSTER A dose of a vaccine given a period after the original vaccine, to 'boost' the effect and maintain immunisation against the disease.

CHOLERA An infection of the intestine, usually caused by contaminated food or water.

COWPOX A viral disease found in cattle; once used to inoculate humans against smallpox.

DNA Deoxyribonucleic acid, a long molecule made from four bases; the nucleic acid in which genetic information is coded.

ENDEMIC A disease that is common and widespread in a population.

EPIDEMIC A disease that breaks out suddenly and without warning, infecting a significant proportion of the population.

FORMALIN A solution in water of formaldehyde, a powerful disinfectant. The strength used to make the poliovirus inactive in a vaccine is 37 per cent (*see* IPV).

GENE Made of DNA, each gene carries information that determines a part of a living organism's characteristics and is passed on to the next generation. Thousands of genes are carried on a chromosome.

GENETIC CODE The sequence of nucleotides along the RNA strand.

HIV Human Immunodeficiency Virus. Many people who are HIV-positive go on to develop the disease AIDS.

IMMUNE SYSTEM The collection of cells and proteins that work to protect the body from harmful micro-organisms.

IMMUNISATION A process that makes someone less likely to catch a disease or infection or, if the infection is caught, makes the disease less dangerous.

INOCULATION The introduction of a pathogen or antigen into the body, especially to stimulate the production of antibodies or other immune responses.

IPV 'Inactive polio vaccine'; a 'killed' polio vaccine made from inactive poliovirus; developed by Jonas Salk and his team.

IRON LUNG A metal cylinder for polio patients unable to breathe on their own. Inside the cylinder the air pressure is varied between high and low, helping to push the chest in and out as in normal breathing.

MICRO-ORGANISM Any organism that can only be seen using a microscope.

OPV 'Oral polio vaccine'; a live polio vaccine; developed by Albert Sabin.

PATHOGEN A micro-organism, including bacteria and viruses, that can cause disease.

PENICILLIN One of a group of antibacterial drugs called antibiotics. Penicillin works by killing the disease-causing bacteria.

PLAGUE A highly infectious disease, resulting in high fever, large pustules and often death.

POLIOMYELITIS The full name for polio, from the Greek words *polios*, meaning 'grey' and *muelos*, meaning 'marrow', referring to the grey substance of the spinal cord.

RNA Ribonucleic acid. Normally RNA converts DNA information into proteins in cells. In viruses, RNA works as a kind of ultra-simple DNA and holds the genetic information.

SMALLPOX A very contagious viral disease, causing high fever and a rash.

SYMPTOM A sign of illness; an indicator that the body is not working properly.

TOXIN A poisonous substance that can cause disease.

TRANSMISSION The passing of information from one cell to another.

TYPHOID FEVER A dangerous infection, spread by contaminated food or water.

VACCINATION A process of administering a vaccine as a precaution against contracting a disease.

VACCINE A virus prepared for the purpose of inoculating humans and other animals to give them immunity to the disease caused by that virus.

VIRUS A micro-organism, associated with disease, made of nucleic acid. A virus has no DNA and cannot live on its own. It must attach itself to a cell to live and reproduce.

WHITE BLOOD CELLS Cells in the blood that are responsible for destroying harmful bacteria, viruses and fungi.

FURTHER INFORMATION

WEB SITES
www.who.int/topics/poliomyelitis/en/
The World Health Organization web site has lots of fascinating information about polio, as well as articles about the progress of the eradication programme it initiated.

www.marchofdimes.com
The home page of the March of Dimes, which came out of Franklin D. Roosevelt's National Foundation for Infantile Paralysis; the site has lots of further information on the history of the organisation and the work it does today.

BOOKS
Jonas Salk – Polio Pioneer by Corinne J. Naden and Rose J. Blue: Gateway Biographies, Millbrook Press, 2001
Jonas Salk and the Polio Vaccine by John Bankston: Mitchell Lane Publishers, 2001
Close to Home: A Story of the Polio Epidemic by Lydia Weaver: Puffin Books, 1997
Polio by Allison Stark Draper: Rosen Publishing Group, 2001
Polio by Alan Hecht and I. Edward Alcamo: Deadly Diseases and Epidemics, Chelsea House Publications, 2003

OTHER SOURCES
All the time, steps are being taken towards eradicating polio from our world. Keep an eye out in newspapers and magazines for articles about vaccination programmes in the developing world.

INDEX

Africa 39, 40
AIDS 41, 45
alchemy 7, 8, 45
ancient Egypt 6, 18
animals 12, 13, 27, 28, 46
anthrax 12
antibiotics 16, 27, 46
antibodies 4 15, 16, 18, 20, 21, 26, 27, 28, 29, 30, 35, 36, 37, 41, 45
antigens 15, 16, 45, 46
antitoxins 10, 45
Australia 23
autism 42, 43, 45
bacteria 10, 12, 13, 14, 15, 16, 27, 45, 46
bioterrorists 41
blindness 4, 7
blood 15
boosters 16, 29, 34, 37, 45
brain 4, 18, 25, 45
Brazil 40
breastfeeding 18, 19
British royal family 9
Canada 20, 34, 35
cells 15, 16, 24, 45, 46
chest muscles 4, 17, 18, 25, 46
chicken cholera 12
Chile 37
China 39
cholera 6, 45
chromosomes 45
contamination 11, 18, 20, 34, 37, 40, 45, 46
cowpox 8, 9, 10, 12, 45
crippled 14, 32
cure 4, 14, 18, 20, 42
Cutter 33, 34
Denmark 28, 44
developed countries 42
developing world 37, 39
digestive system 15, 36
diphtheria 10, 13, 14, 28, 37, 42
DNA (deoxyribonucleic acid) 15, 45
Dominican Republic 39
donations 5, 23, 28
dosage 4, 16, 21, 26
DPT immunisation 37
Eisenhower, Dwight D. 36
endemic 39, 40, 45
Enders team 34, 37
Enders, John F. 27, 44
epidemics and outbreaks 4, 14, 17, 18, 19, 20, 21, 25, 28, 34, 35, 37, 40, 41, 43, 44, 45
Europe 21, 25, 29, 38, 39
fermentation 12, 13
fever 8, 18, 46
First World War 21

foot-and-mouth 13
formaldehyde 10, 45
formalin 10, 26, 28, 44, 45
Francis, Thomas 24
fundraising 21, 22, 23
genes 45
genetic code 41, 45
Great Britain 10, 12, 23, 42, 44
Guillain-Barré Syndrome 23
Hahnemann, Samuel 8, 9, 10
Haiti 39
Hall, Jeff 38
headaches 7, 8, 18
HIV 15, 21, 41, 45
hospitals 20, 23, 32, 42
human body 4, 15, 16, 17
immune system 15, 16, 21, 23, 41, 45
immunisation 10, 11, 32, 33, 36, 37, 42, 43, 44, 45, 46
immunity 8, 10, 14, 16, 29, 35, 36, 40
India 38, 39, 40
infection 6, 10, 12, 13, 17, 40, 44, 46
influenza 15, 21, 24, 41
inoculation 5, 9, 12, 38, 46
intestines 17, 35, 36, 37, 45
IPV (inactive polio vaccine) 10, 13, 26, 28, 29, 32, 33, 35, 40, 44, 46
iron lungs 4, 17, 18, 32, 46
Japan 37
Jenner, Edward 4, 6, 8, 9, 10, 11, 12, 13, 42, 44
Kelly, Grace 22
Kenny, Sister Elizabeth 23
killed-virus vaccine *see* IPV
Kolmer, John 22
Koprowski, Hilary 29
Landsteiner, Karl 19, 44
Law of Similars 8, 9
live-virus vaccine *see* OPV
malaria 7, 8
March of Dimes 22, 23
Mary II, Queen 7
mass-vaccination 34, 38, 40, 42, 44
measles 37, 43
medical history 10, 24
medicine 6, 7
Mexico 37
micro-organisms 12, 13, 14, 16, 24, 38, 45, 46
microscopes 7, 13, 14, 46
Middle East 40
MMR (measles-mumps rubella) 37, 42, 43
molecule 45
monkeys 19, 27, 28, 29, 44
Montagu, Lady Mary Wortley 9, 44
Morgan, Dr Isabel 26, 44
mumps 35

muscles 19, 23
mutation 38, 39, 41
National Foundation for Infantile Paralysis (NFIP) 5, 22, 23, 24, 44
National Immunisation Days 40
Nelmes, Sarah 10
nervous system 17, 35
Netherlands 37
New York 18, 19, 20, 21, 33, 34
New York University School of Medicine 26
Nigeria 40, 44
Nobel Prize for Medicine 34
nucleic acid 14, 45, 46
nucleotides 45
opium 7
OPV (oral polio vaccine) 26, 28, 32, 33, 35, 36, 37, 38, 40, 43, 44, 46
organisms 14, 15
Paracelsus 7, 8
paralysis 4, 17, 18, 19, 20, 22, 23, 25, 37, 41
parasites 15
Pasteur, Louis 12, 13
pathogens 46
penicillin 27, 46
Phipps, James 10
plague 6, 7, 46
poliomyelitis 14, 17, 46
    cases worldwide 39
    containment of 17
    effects of 42
    eradication of 5, 36, 38, 39, 40, 42, 43, 44
    victims of 18, 23, 30
poliovirus 14, 17, 18, 19, 21, 22, 24, 25, 26, 27, 28, 29, 33, 35, 36, 37, 40, 41, 43, 44, 45
    types of 5, 19, 22, 25, 26, 28, 29, 41, 44
post-polio syndrome 42
prevention 6, 14, 42
proteins 45, 46
Public Health Service, US 21
pustules 12, 46
quarantine 21
quinine 8
rabies 12
Rainier III, Prince of Monaco 22
research 5, 12, 22, 24, 25, 26, 27, 41, 43, 44
RNA (ribonucleic acid) 15, 45, 46
Roosevelt, Franklin D. 5, 22, 23, 24, 31, 44
rubella 37
Sabin, Albert 5, 26, 34, 35, 36, 37, 38, 40, 43, 44, 46
Salk, Jonas 4, 23, 24, 25, 26, 27, 28, 29, 30, 31,

32, 33, 34, 35, 36, 37, 38, 40, 44, 46
sanitation 14, 17, 20, 35
Scandinavia 18
Second World War 24
side-effects 31
Siptah, Pharaoh 19
smallpox 4, 6, 7, 8, 9, 10, 11, 12, 26, 42, 44, 45, 46
Soviet Union 37
spinal cord 18, 27, 46
Sweden 37
swimming pools 20
symptoms 8, 9, 10, 17, 18, 23, 25, 46
syphilis 7
Temple University Medical School, Pennsylvania 22
terrorists 41
tetanus 37
tissue 17, 18, 19, 21, 23, 27, 28, 30, 34, 37, 44
toxin 10, 46
transmission 46
treatment 4, 6, 8, 19
trials 9, 29, 30, 31, 32, 37, 44
Turkey 8, 9, 44
typhoid fever 14, 46
University of Cincinnati College of Medicine 35
University of Michigan 24
University of New York 41
University of Pittsburgh School of Medicine, USA 24, 44
USA 4, 20, 21, 23, 24, 26, 27, 28, 29, 30, 31, 32, 33, 35, 36, 37, 39, 44
vaccination 8, 9, 12, 22, 42, 43, 46
    effectiveness 34
    kits 5, 38
    made compulsory 11, 12
    programmes 5, 31, 36, 37, 38, 42, 43, 44
variolation 8, 9, 10, 11, 12, 44
Varro, Marcus Terrentius 7
viruses 4, 5, 14, 15, 16, 17, 24, 26, 37, 45, 46
    filter-passing 13
    growth 16
    reproduction 15, 17
water therapy 19
Weaver, Harry 24
Weller, Thomas 27
white blood cells 15, 16, 41, 45
whooping cough 37
William II, King 7
Wimmer, Eckhard 41
World Health Organization (WHO) 7, 42, 43, 44
Wyeth drug company 31